CW00802647

LAZY LAMA LOOKS AT

Loving Kindness

Our true brave heart

RINGU TULKU RINPOCHE

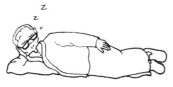

Number 7 in the Lazy Lama series

Bodhicharya
PUBLICATIONS
Awaken the heart by opening the mind

First Published in 2017 by Bodhicharya Publications
Bodhicharya Publications is a Community Interest Company
registered in the UK.
38 Moreland Avenue, Hereford, HR1 1BN, UK
www.bodhicharya.org   email: publications@bodhicharya.org

ISBN 978-0-9957343-0-2

Compiled by Margaret Ford.
Original transcripts by Jet Mort and Margaret Ford.
Editing by Margaret Ford, Mary Heneghan and Maeve O'Sullivan.

Typesetting & Design by Paul O'Connor at Judo Design, Ireland.

Printed on recycled paper by Imprint Digital, Devon, UK.

Cover Image: iStockphoto
Lazy Lama logo: Conrad Harvey & Rebecca O'Connor

Editor's Preface

In March 2011 I took early retirement from my paid employment with the Scottish Government. It had been my plan to concentrate on the work I had been doing for Ringu Tulku and Bodhicharya and I also hoped to be able to give more time to Buddhist study and practice. However, as often happens in life, those plans were taken away from me when I became ill with an auto-immune condition. Instead of doing more for Bodhicharya, I gradually had to give it all up. As the condition worsened, I was hardly able to leave home except for doctor's appointments. Chronic fatigue and inflammation in my eyes meant that I had problems reading and staying awake.

In such circumstances, with twenty or so years of Buddhist study and practice behind me, some people may have imagined that I could have turned towards even more practice. What else could I do? But, to be honest, that was furthest from my mind. I just wanted to sleep and be free from pain.

It was only in the Spring of 2012 that the condition gradually improved and flowed into remission and I began to believe that I was going to get my life back again. It was also then, after those dark months of illness, that I came to see that I had come through it all, not from something I had done, not from some divine intervention, not from some miracle drug, but solely because of the love and kindness of others. It had been the little things: the cup of tea my husband would bring me every morning before he went to work, the meals he cooked for me trying to encourage me to eat, the baths he ran, the stories he would read to me from the newspapers and internet. It had been the phone calls and visits from my children and sisters and close friends. It was simply that I'd been fortunate enough to have people around me who cared. Not since childhood had I been cared for so much. I'd experienced the true meaning of what Rinpoche says in these teachings: *'We live by the love of others.'*

For some, these teachings on loving kindness may seem simple and obvious. But, if we try to understand them deeply, and if we can take them to heart, then I believe that they may be profoundly life-changing. I do hope this book will be of benefit to many people and that it will help encourage us all to develop and live with a brave heart of loving kindness and compassion.

Margaret Ford
Bodhicharya Publications
Scotland, December 2016

Kindness

The teachings of the Buddha encourage us to really welcome loving kindness, to welcome compassion. This is the whole point of the teachings. 'Compassion' is an English translation of what we call *karuna* in Sanskrit, but compassion may not be the best or only word to describe what is being encouraged here. When I looked it up in the English dictionary, to be compassionate seems to mean 'to suffer together' or 'to suffer with.' If you understand compassion like that, then maybe you wouldn't want to welcome it. I know that I don't want to suffer, and I don't want to suffer together or with anyone else. So maybe compassion is not the best translation.

I feel that 'kindness' is an easier word to understand, it is clearer. The main practice, and the main understanding, is to learn to have a benevolent feeling towards everybody. That is compassion or loving kindness. It's to *not* have malevolent feelings towards or against anybody. It's to *not* have angry, harmful, violent, unkind feelings against anybody, but to feel genuinely kind, benevolent and warm towards everybody.

All we need is love

It's a biological thing that we need love. We need care, we need contact with somebody. As we grow, we need to be touched, we need to be cared for, we need to be hugged and that is a biological need. If we don't have that, then we do not grow to become healthy. It is therefore not just psychological or emotional, but it is also physical, biological. We need love, everybody needs love and we learn how to love by receiving love from others. We all want to be cared for and loved and we want to give love also. Actually, the whole of human society lives by the love of others.

So, we all need love, and we should all express our love, our kindness and compassion. But why are we not able to do that? If everybody has love and everybody needs love, then why are people not loving and kind and compassionate all the time? It's because we have lots of negative emotions; we have lots of fear, we have insecurity, we have confusion. We have hatred and anger and too much greed. We also maybe make our love a little tainted so that it becomes attachment, and then it becomes very difficult for ourselves and for others. So, we need to learn to deal with our emotions.

Emotions

From the Buddhist point of view, we try to distinguish between negative emotions and positive emotions. Negative emotions are emotions that bring pain to myself. And, because of that, if I have too much pain, I cause harm to others.

Positive emotions are emotions that make me more joyful and kinder. If I have those emotions, they will result in my actions being of help and benefit to others. Those are positive emotions.

Negative emotions are things like anger, hatred and aversion. They are regarded as negative because, if I am very angry then I am feeling bad and, as long as I hold on to emotions like that, then I am disturbed and very unhappy. And, if I express those emotions, I will harm others because there is a malevolent feeling to anger.

But then, there are other emotions like too much greed, too much craving and clinging, which are also regarded as negative emotions - because they create feelings of dissatisfaction. I feel I don't have enough and I need, and want, more and more. Being greedy means I have a sense of dissatisfaction and unhappiness. And this unhappiness leads to actions that will harm people, because I will create situations where I want things or I take things, whether people offer them to me or not, willingly or not. And then also there are emotions like too much arrogance and too much jealousy. All of these things are also regarded as negative emotions.

Now, what is the opposite of these? What are the positive emotions? If you look at positive emotions, or the other side of these negative emotions, it will not be so difficult to find that actually the opposite, or the positive side of all these, is one thing: loving kindness. If you are angry, you have negative feelings against somebody and you want to harm them. But, if you have loving kindness and compassion, a good heart, you will want to wish others to be well. It is the direct opposite of anger.

Even if we look at greed, we might say that the opposite is generosity. But, where is the generosity coming from? It is from compassion, from loving kindness, from a benevolent feeling towards others.

It is the same with jealousy. If someone has something good and I feel bad about that, then that is jealousy. But the opposite is rejoicing if somebody else has something good. It is being happy for them.

So therefore, from a Buddhist point of view, if we can generate and cultivate loving kindness or compassion then that will help reduce our negative feelings. This one positive emotion is enough to balance out all others.

Let the love grow

When we try to generate loving kindness or compassion, even a little bit, we will feel peaceful, joyful and happy. I have never heard anyone say, 'Oh, I was so happy this morning because I was so angry!' To be angry is to be unhappy. If I feel loving, if I feel kind, I will feel good because it is a warm feeling. And when I'm in that state of mind, I'm light, I'm joyful, I'm smiling. I can be nice to everybody and I am not suffering.

And, if more and more people feel like that, most of the time, then the world can become like a heaven. Sometimes, we feel that things are so difficult and it's impossible to change the world because the world is in so much trouble. There are so many problems, difficulties and conflicts; so much violence. But, if most of the people in the world started to be kind to each other, today; tomorrow, the world would be a wonderful place to live. We can imagine that, it's easy to imagine that. We don't need much. We only need people to be kind to each other.

An exercise on love

There are practices - sometimes we call them meditations or practices or exercises - which are about feeling and generating loving kindness. One exercise is done like this:

think about someone whom you love very much, like your child, your parent or your friend. Someone you really love. And feel how much you wish that person to be well. You think and feel how much happiness you want for them and about how strong your love is for them. You keep generating that feeling.

Then, after some time of doing this, think of someone else whom you also have close feelings for, but who is not as close to you as the first person. Try to feel for them as you did for that first person whom you loved so much. Try to wish them the same happiness as you did for the first person.

In this way, you can slowly extend this feeling to other people around you, those close to you and those not so close. You can try to feel the same loving kindness and compassion for all of them as you did for that first person whom you love so much. This is because we are all basically the same. As much as I wish to be happy and joyful and well, everybody also wishes that. So, why not wish them all well? Why not wish that they all be free from pain and suffering and troubles? Just as I wish for myself and for those close to me.

Then the practice is to extend this feeling to people throughout the country, throughout the world. Feel as if you are really radiating love and kindness to all.

A happy life

Through doing this practice, even if I cannot generate a feeling of universal love and compassion, I can still benefit myself. Because I will feel good in my heart, I will feel warm in my heart and I will feel good. And if I do something inspired by that love and kindness and compassion I am feeling, I would be doing something that would be beneficial or helpful to someone else. I don't know anyone who would not feel proud of themselves or good in themselves in doing that. I would feel I have done something useful and meaningful and I can be happy about that and I can love myself more.

So, actually, the best way of loving myself is by doing something compassionate. If I love myself and I am proud of myself then I am living a meaningful life. And if I feel that my life is meaningful, my life is useful, that my life is of value, then I'm living a good life, a proper life and therefore a happy life.

At the same time, I'm not doing anything

bad to anyone and I'm only trying to help. If I'm living a life that's good for myself and is good for others, then what is better than that? And especially if that love, that compassion, that kindness extends to more and more people and if I can even extend that to everybody, then it's even more ideal, it's much better. I would be thinking about doing something good, something useful, something meaningful for anybody and everybody, and I will do that with happiness, with joy and with willingness, because I know that it is something that is good for me too.

When kindness heals

I was in America last year and I met a young lady there who told me a story and I thought it was very interesting. She said that she had lots of difficulties in her life at that time and she was very low with depression and she had no job. One day she was driving someone's pick-up truck and she was in the gas station and backed up and had an accident. She ran into a very posh car and damaged it quite a lot. And she had nothing, no insurance, nothing. So, she was totally shocked and came out of her car saying, 'What am I to do now? What to do?'

Then a nice, elderly lady came out of the car and said to her, 'Don't worry too much. Don't worry, you don't need to call the police. We can work it out between ourselves.' The younger lady told her that she had no insurance. But the older lady simply replied, 'We can work out something. Just give me your telephone number and we can discuss what to do.'

Two days later, she got a telephone call from the older lady who told her she had been looking for a garage to repair the car and they had asked for $2,000 but she said she thought she could find something better. And then, after another two days, she called again and said, 'I think I have found the solution. I got my car repaired by someone for $500 so you don't have to worry. If you have money, you can pay me back in instalments. But if you can't, it's okay, don't bother.'

The young lady told me that the incident healed her. She said before that she had been in very bad shape. She was upset, had depression and she was so unhappy she was seeing everything as very dark and dismal. Nothing seemed good in the world. But, after just meeting this one very nice, kind lady, the world looked good again. 'Afterwards the world seemed not so bad, it's quite okay,' she said. She got her confidence back and all her depression disappeared and she felt her world to be completely different.

So, it's like this sometimes: just because of one kind person or one kind act, everything can change. This was actually not a great thing to happen, it was not what the young woman would have wanted to happen, it was an accident. But because of how this one person reacted, it affected the other person in a very good way.

The brave heart

In Buddhist teachings, we have the concept of a Bodhisattva. Sometimes they call it a compassionate warrior, or a warrior of compassion. A knight – like in the stories of King Arthur and the Knights of the Round Table – but fighting for lasting peace and happiness for all beings. So many stories and movies, like King Arthur or Braveheart or Star Wars... they are all based on this kind of an idea, of a good side fighting a bad side. The idea of a Bodhisattva is just the same but it is more about being a 'warrior of compassion' than being a 'compassionate warrior,' because it's about being a champion of good, rather than fighting with swords. A Bodhisattva is a true brave heart; one who saves others, like Braveheart in the story, but not through killing others.

I recently saw a quote on the internet saying that 'a Bodhisattva is an ordinary person who acts like an adult.' In a way, I think that is true. A Bodhisattva is an ordinary person who tries to do good things for themselves and for others.

So, how can I become a Bodhisattva or a brave heart? It's a problem if we think of a Bodhisattva as someone unusual and extraordinary like Superman or Superwoman. I don't think we should see it like that. Rather, we should think that becoming a Bodhisattva is possible for any of us. Of course, there are different levels of Bodhisattvas, but at the level we are right now, we can also be a Bodhisattva, a brave heart, and generate compassion. We do not need to be super-human or extraordinary.

One time when I was talking to a group of students, I was asking them how many of them felt that they were Bodhisattvas. Almost no one said that they were. Perhaps they felt it would be too grand a claim to say so. But I feel that is not right. We have to feel that we are Bodhisattvas. Just 'an ordinary person who acts like an adult,' that is not so extraordinary

We are beginners

Of course, we can have high ideals, and it is very important to understand that. Because then we know where to aim and in which direction we need to develop our motivation, compassion and wisdom. But I don't need to think I cannot be a Bodhisattva if I do not have the high, ideal experience of compassion and wisdom of a great Bodhisattva. While we have to understand and have some knowledge of the ideal, we also have to understand and know that we are not at that ideal stage. We are beginners and we should work at that stage. It is okay to accept where we are. You cannot have a school without a first grade, after all. Whatever level we are at, we should try to do our best. And in this way, we are practising the path of the Bodhisattva.

There are two levels of understanding: there is the ideal, and there is my own level, my own situation. If I cannot accept my own level, I cannot progress, because I cannot be something I am not. If I can work at my level, even a little bit, and remind myself how I should be feeling and reacting and what would be best for me and best for others at that level, I can still be and think and feel that I am working on the path of a Bodhisattva. I need to train myself gradually, step by step.

Compassion

As I mentioned before, I'm not sure if compassion is the best word to use in English, because it's not clear to me how people understand compassion generally. Compassion is basically understood from the Buddhist point of view as wishing to free others from suffering. It is knowing, from my own experience, that suffering is not nice or good and that, therefore, I want to free myself from suffering and so I also want to free others from suffering. Compassion is really wishing people to be free from suffering. Not only that, you not only wish them to be free from suffering, but you also wish them to become very happy and to have the highest wellbeing.

That is compassion.

We need to understand compassion and the benefits of compassion; that is very important. We also need to understand the benefits of developing wisdom and compassion within ourselves: slowly but surely increasing our own compassionate attitude and compassionate way of acting and reacting in our lives. This is the essence of Buddhist teachings, but you don't need to call it 'Buddhism.' It is also the essence of becoming a good human being.

If you wish to give it a name, you could call it Bodhicitta. And if you don't want to give it a name like that, then you could call it compassion. You could call it a good heart. You can call it anything you like. And it is said clearly again and again: you don't need to be a Buddhist to be a Bodhisattva. But, if you are a Bodhisattva in your heart, from the Buddhist point of view, then you are a very good Buddhist.

Not a doormat

Sometimes people have the misunderstanding that, if I have compassion, then I have to do everything that anyone asks me to do or wishes me to do; that I can't say no and I have to become a slave. That is why some people think that being compassionate is very difficult. But it's not like that. It is more that I try to be compassionate but that doesn't mean that I have to do everything that anyone asks me to do.

Actually, I should *not* be doing everything that anyone asks me to do, even if I have the power to do it. If something is helpful and good for others, now and in the long run, then I can try to help them in that way. If it is not, then I don't have to do it. Also, how much I can do depends on different situations. Even if I can't do anything now, I can still have a good wish, at least a positive intention, so that I mean well and have a benevolent feeling. That does not ask too much. That doesn't make you feel like a doormat. If anyone has compassion, it is only good. I can't see anything wrong, or any downside, of feeling compassion.

Being kind to myself

Feeling compassion is not only wishing well and feeling good for others, but also feeling good for myself. If I don't wish well for myself, then I can't wish well for others, because I wouldn't know that they would need that. If I didn't know that I want to be free from suffering, why would I want others to be free from suffering? If I didn't wish that I could have happiness and joy and positive things, then I wouldn't know that others would want these things too. So, when I wish others to be free from suffering that is based on my own experience of wishing to be free from suffering. So, the first step is to wish myself to be free from suffering and to have wellbeing and happiness and all positive things.

It is possible that, if you really see the wellbeing of others as very important, then you can sacrifice yourself, your pleasure, or your own happiness to bring a lot of happiness and good things for others. That is possible, but it has to be done of your own free will. You have to do that with happiness and with willingness. You do it with pride.

Compassion is like that: I wish well for myself and therefore wish well for others. I wish to be free from suffering, I wish everyone to be free from suffering because we are all in the same boat in wanting these things. And, whether you want to call it compassion or you call it love, whether you want to call it kindness or whatever, it is our natural feeling and we all have it.

Not only human beings, other animals also have that love. I've heard that many animals even have the capacity to sacrifice their lives for others. Furthermore, they found that those animals that do such altruistic things are not stupid animals. The more intelligent they are, the more altruistic they will be. So, having compassion is not a sign of stupidity, it is a sign of intelligence, and also of courage and clarity.

Go see your mother

There is a story that I often tell because I think it is very important. It is about the great master, Patrul Rinpoche, and a young monk who came to study with him, who was very bright and intelligent. One day Patrul Rinpoche asked him, 'Do you miss your mother?' The young monk replied, 'No, I don't miss my mother. I'm a monk, I don't miss her at all.' Patrul Rinpoche said, 'Oh, that is so sad - you don't understand anything! You have got it all totally wrong. So from today you can just stop all the things you are doing. Stop all your studies and meditations and just think about your mother, and how kind and nice she is.'

So the young monk did that. He thought about his mother and, the more he thought about her, the more he missed her. After a few days he was missing her so much that he began to cry and he couldn't bear it. He went to Patrul Rinpoche and said that he missed his mother so much that he couldn't do without seeing her. He said, 'Can't I go home and be with my mother for a little bit?'

Patrul Rinpoche replied, 'If you have no love or gratitude or don't miss your mother how can you be compassionate? How can you be a good practitioner? So, yes, go and be with your mother. Then when you come back, you will understand.' The young monk went to see his mother and later he returned, but his connection with his mother was always there and he always missed his mother from then on.

Secular ethics

His Holiness the Dalai Lama is trying very hard to try to formulate and make public what he calls 'secular ethics.' Actually what he means is kindness and compassion and that everybody should regard compassion as something that is useful and valuable and needed, whether you belong to any religion or any spiritual group or none. That's why he calls it secular because it's nothing to do with any kind of belief system.

If you have the understanding that loving kindness and compassion are something really needed and useful for human beings, for us, for each other and for the whole world, then you have something really valuable. If you have this understanding, you will be nice and kind to each other and you won't need anything else. You won't need rules, you won't need laws, because you will follow your heart and you will follow the right path.

But, if the understanding of the value of loving kindness and compassion is not there, then, no matter how many rules and laws there are, they will only be broken because there is no heart.

If we really have that understanding and clarity, then we will naturally generate loving kindness and compassion and we will naturally react with loving kindness and compassion. And, the more we naturally react like that, then the more we will know the negativity or the fault of feeling the opposite.

The thorny differences

Of course, life is not a bed of roses, and even roses have their thorns. Life is a challenge, the world is a challenge and there are lots of problems and suffering. We human beings have some good things but also shortcomings: ignorance and misunderstandings. We have 'un-clarity.' We have many negative emotions and habits.

We are, in many ways, very different from each other. We have different ways of thinking, different ways of doing things, different ways of seeing things. Even people within Europe can be very different. In the beginning, I thought that everyone who had yellow hair was the same! Actually, at first I thought that all human beings were the same. In a way it's true - at a certain level we are all the same. There is no one who doesn't want to be free from suffering, pain and problems. There is no one who doesn't have some kind of love, kindness and compassion; and no one who doesn't want happiness and joy. We all have the same basic emotions. But there is a thin layer of culture on the top of that and that is where the differences are. And sometimes these superficial differences give rise to conflict or misunderstanding.

The wish-fulfilling gem

The whole point is that, if we want a really happy world, a good world, a wonderful world, we need compassion. If we want a good family, we need compassion. And for ourselves too, we need compassion - to love myself, to be happy, to feel good about myself, I need compassion. Therefore, we can try to generate more compassion and understanding of the importance of compassion. Also, we can try to understand that there is absolutely no downside to feeling compassionate, because everybody wants love and wants to feel love. We all want this.

If you can feel kindness from others and if you can feel kindness in your heart, you will feel good. And if you do something useful and beneficial, not only is it benefitting others, but it benefits yourself also. That is why, in Buddhist teachings, they say that compassion is like a wish-fulfilling gem. If you have that feeling and the more you have that, it's good for you and good for others. It's good for now and good in the long run. Once you have loving kindness and compassion, and that feeling increases, then all positive things can grow. It is like a jewel that can fulfil all wishes.

Discussion

Questioner: Rinpoche, you talked about the 'ideal' and also how we can practise loving kindness and compassion as a beginner. I find that whatever little glimpse of compassion I have is always rooted in my own agenda of how to fix things. If I am going to wait until I reach that ideal it will take a long time. So, can I really help people with this ego type compassion while aspiring to the ideal?

Rinpoche: Yes, that's the idea. The understanding is that we don't have to wait for anything, we just have to start now because whatever little compassion we have is mixed up with lots of obscurations and shortcomings and weaknesses and attachments. We have to work on them. Compassion that is full of wisdom is a possibility, it is an ideal but we should never wait for the ideal. We have to start from where we are. So, actually, it almost can't be ideal. If you can do everything perfectly just now then you don't need to practise because you are already enlightened! All practice is therefore working from where you are. Even a little bit of compassion is good. A little bit more is even better. Of course, this does not mean that you should not improve. It's not saying that if you have some compassion then you should keep it just like that. But, it's good enough. And then you work on it, that's the understanding. That's the practice.

It's very important to accept where you are and what you are. To understand what capacity you have or how advanced you are. That's the first thing. If you have lots of problems and negative emotions and lots of ignorance, you have to accept that. 'Accepting' meaning that you have to be okay with it. You cannot imagine you are someone or something else and work on that, you cannot do that. You cannot expect to be as if all the problems and weaknesses are not there and practise from that. So, you really have to face who and what and where you are. And this is sometimes difficult because we do not want to see the way we are. We also can't see our enlightened aspect, our Buddha nature, and that's another matter. But it is very important to understand that we need to face our weaknesses and problems, we need to acknowledge them. 'This is what I am; I am like this.' Then I can practise and improve because that is the basis from a Buddhist point of view. I can improve, step by step.

Questioner: I love the phrase you used, 'We live by the love of others.' Can you say something more about this?

Rinpoche: So, we human beings live by the love of others, and even during that short time when we are supposed to be independent, when we are grown up and healthy, we are still dependent. We still need the love of others, we need the appreciation of others and we need the help and support of others. If we don't support and help each other we will get nothing done. We can't be successful or happy; we can't progress. It's like the saying: *'When the trees support each other then we have houses and cities, when human beings support each other we have society, we have civilization.'* So, the whole of society, of civilization, survives by supporting and helping each other.

It's very important to understand this, we are dependent on the love of others and because of this we can grow. It's not only when we are born, or when we are dying, but also the time in between. When we really understand this then we know that we have to do the same for others. And when I do something good and useful and beneficial, I am doing it for myself and also for my society, for my people. It is not just for me, but it's for 'we.'

There is another saying in India that goes like this: *'For the sake of the world, one must sacrifice one's country. For the sake of one's country, one must sacrifice one's village. For the sake of the village, one must sacrifice one's family. And for the sake of one's family, one must sacrifice oneself."*

The world is most important because it includes us all, our country, our village, our family, myself. So, if the world is going badly then how can things be good for my country and village and family? But unfortunately, nowadays, this is often seen in reverse, in a materialistic and egotistical way, where people sacrifice their families for themselves. They sacrifice their village and country for themselves and sometimes the world for their own gain. But this is idiotic! How can I really have anything good, how can I be happy if everyone else is in bad shape? So, the most important thing to understand and remember is how dependent we all are on each other. And it's not like a business transaction where, if I do something good then I get something back. It is knowing that if I do something beneficial for others, for my society, then I am doing something good and something meaningful.

Questioner: Could you say something about the dedication of merit in relation to this?

Rinpoche: In Buddhism, everything has a beginning, middle and an end. The beginning is the aspiration or motivation. The middle is doing something positive. And the end is the dedication. The aspiration is thinking about what is the most important thing for me. I want to have everlasting peace and happiness and to be free from suffering and everyone is just like me and they want the same. So, my aspiration is a wish to do something towards that; to bring an end to everyone's suffering and a wish for everlasting peace and happiness for everybody. Whatever practice I am about to do, or whatever positive deed I intend to do will contribute towards that end. So, that is the aspiration. It is said that any action that you do can be considered good or bad, depending on your motivation. How can this be? For example, if I give a talk on Dharma then it might be seen as a good thing to do. But, if my motivation is to make myself popular or to make money from the people there, then giving that talk is not good. My agenda is not good. Sometimes we start with a good motivation and become corrupted, that happens easily. So we have to remind ourselves, again and again, of our positive aspirations to help myself and to help others to have everlasting happiness and to be free from suffering.

Then I do my practice, or some positive deed, and after that I do the dedication. Now, the dedication is very important and, from a Buddhist point of view, if you have done something good but you make a bad dedication, then the result can be very negative. So you must make a good and limitless dedication because making a strong dedication is the way to multiply your positive deeds. If you say that the dedication is to get rid of someone's headache, it might get rid of the headache, but then all the power of the positive deed is finished. Instead, if you say that the positive deed is to help all beings become enlightened, with everlasting peace and happiness, and to be free from suffering, and to get rid of their headache, then the headache might go but also the power of the dedication will not finish until all the other things happen too. It is therefore important to have a very big dedication!

You can make a dedication by saying something like this:

'This practice, this positive deed, whatever I did, together with all the positive things I've done in all my past, all the positive things I'm doing now in this life, and all the positive things I will do in the future, I dedicate all of these together for all beings.'

That's how it's done and it is a skilful way of dedicating because nothing is wasted and all the merit from the positive deed or practice or meditation is multiplied.

Questioner: Rinpoche, I understand that meditation can help us work on our negative emotions and develop compassion and wisdom. Could you please give us some meditation instructions?

Rinpoche: So, practically, if we are doing sitting meditation, we relax our body. Try to let all tensions go because we don't want them. Relax our body from our toes to our head, to the brain, to the eyes. Relax. Wherever there is tension, we try to relax. Relax our eyes. Relax our face muscles, our mouth, neck, shoulders and internal organs. Relax our feet, our hands. We really relax our whole body. And bring our mind into the body so that I feel the body. I am here. I am now, in my body. I feel the relax-ness of my body, I see with my eyes, I hear what I hear with my ears, I feel with my body, I smell with my nose. So I am here now, in this very moment. I am not there in yesterday, I am not there in tomorrow, and I am here in my body now, this moment.

My mind is also relaxed. I am not dealing

with all the problems from yesterday, I am not dealing with the problems of tomorrow, I am not even dealing with the problems of the last hour or minute or the next hour or minute. I am just here, now.

Only seeing what I am seeing, now. Only hearing what I am hearing, now. Not holding on to anybody or anything, just being.

I am not meditating. I am not doing anything, I am just being. Clear, open, not fighting against anything, not closing anything, not trying to wish away anything, not trying to get anything. Just here being natural.

Maybe a thought comes, it doesn't matter. You hear something, it doesn't matter. You see something, it doesn't matter. Whatever you see, it's okay. Don't make a story of it. Sometimes a bird sings. Then you think, 'Oh, the bird is singing. It's disturbing me. It has to sing as soon as I start to meditate!' You don't have to think like that. You let the sound come and go and if it continuously comes, continuously let it come and let it go.

With thoughts it is the same. When a thought comes, it's okay. If a thought comes, don't concentrate on the thought, just be in the present moment. And then, if too many thoughts come, allow your mind to be aware of your breathing. You are feeling that you are breathing in. You are breathing in and then you are feeling that you are breathing out. You are not thinking about it, you are just doing it; you are feeling it. If too many thoughts and too many things are going on in your mind then just lightly focus on your breathing because that is what is happening now.

You are not trying to push away thoughts. You are just letting them go, because you are more focused on what is happening now.

You may remember something that happened yesterday. You don't go through it too much, you just remember breathing now.

If you are a little bit more advanced, then you can even look at that thought.

The thought is not a story; it's just a thought coming up. There is nowhere that it comes from, there is nowhere it goes away to. As soon as it arises, it changes. It goes. Another thought comes. And actually that's your mind. There is nothing called one mind. It's the stringing of thoughts and emotions and arisings. It's not one thing.

And all these thoughts and emotions and sensations that arise in your mind are yourself, your mind. It's not coming at you. It's not coming to affect you. That is me, that is my mind. So, therefore, I don't have to be afraid of that. I don't have to be afraid of my fear as well, because that's also myself. Anger, upset, is myself, it's my own manifestation. So there is no need to get rid of it, there's no need to follow it, there is no need to be afraid of it, there's no need to feel bad, or good. I just allow it to be and then, like the waves coming and going, it dissolves itself. There is nothing outside my mind.

So whatever comes, nice experiences,

not nice experiences, they come and they go. And I have to allow them to come and allow them to go. Not holding on to anything, whether good or bad. Even good and bad is just a concept. If I can enjoy myself in all these thoughts and emotions, if I can just relax in my thoughts and emotions, if nothing is happening, it's very nice. It's peaceful; it's joyful. If thoughts and emotions are coming, it's very nice. It comes and it goes and I just relax in it. I don't own it, I don't grab it, I don't build a story on it, I just be… and relax.

If you are trying to meditate for a session, keep an alarm clock. Don't say, 'I want to meditate for five minutes' and look at your watch 50 times. When the time is ended, the alarm clock will come and you might jump out of the meditation! But try not to jump out of it.

Enjoy it. Make friends with your meditation. Think that this is time off. Sometimes you get time off from work, but you don't get time off from your mind. You don't get time off from your thoughts and emotions. This is the only time you can get time off from your thoughts and emotions. So it is real time off. Look forward to that time off. It's not only that you don't have to work but you don't have to think also. It's really the greatest pleasure.

Thank you

All my babbling,
In the name of Dharma
Has been set down faithfully
By my dear students of pure vision.

I pray that at least a fraction of the wisdom
Of those enlightened teachers
Who tirelessly trained me
Shines through this mass of incoherence.

May the sincere efforts of all those
Who have worked tirelessly
Result in spreading the true meaning of
Dharma
To all who are inspired to know.

May this help dispel the darkness of ignorance
In the minds of all living beings
And lead them to complete realisation
Free from all fear.

Ringu Tulku

Acknowledgements

This small book has only been made possible because of the efforts of many people.

We compiled and edited excerpts from talks and teachings given by Ringu Tulku Rinpoche in a number of places over the last few years and we would like to thank the organisers of those talks.

In no particular order, our grateful thanks to: Dzogchen Beara in County Cork, Ireland, for the teachings on Bodhicitta. Rigul Trust in Southampton, England, for the talk on Generating Kindness. Glasgow Samye Dzong, Scotland, for the teachings on Relative Bodhicitta. Bodhicharya Study group, Helsinki, Finland, for the talk on Kindness.

Thank you to our proof readers: Mariette van Lieshout and Peter Ford. Thank you to Jet Mort for the original transcript of the Southampton talk.

Thank you to Mary Heneghan for her

further editing and advice. Thank you also to Maeve O'Sullivan for further editing and proof reading. Thank you to Rachel Moffitt for all her diligent work for Bodhicharya Publications. And to Paul O'Connor for his beautiful layout and design.

Thank you Vicki McKenna for your support and encouragement and friendship and editorial advice.

And finally, many thanks and love to Ringu Tulku Rinpoche for allowing us to share his words on loving kindness and compassion here.

About the Author

Ringu Tulku Rinpoche is a Tibetan Buddhist Master of the Kagyu Order. He was trained in all schools of Tibetan Buddhism under many great masters including HH the 16th Gyalwang Karmapa and HH Dilgo Khyentse Rinpoche. He took his formal education at Namgyal Institute of Tibetology, Sikkim and Sampurnananda Sanskrit University, Varanasi, India. He served as Tibetan Textbook Writer and Professor of Tibetan Studies in Sikkim for 25 years.

Since 1990, he has been travelling and teaching Buddhism and meditation in Europe, America, Canada, Australia and Asia. He participates in various interfaith and 'Science and Buddhism' dialogues and is the author of several books on Buddhist topics. These include Path to Buddhahood, Daring Steps, The Ri-me Philosophy of Jamgon Kongtrul the Great, Confusion Arises as Wisdom, the Lazy Lama series and the Heart Wisdom series, as well as several children's books, available in Tibetan and European languages.

He founded the organisations:
    Bodhicharya - see www.bodhicharya.org
    and Rigul Trust - see www.rigultrust.org

Rigul Trust is a registered UK Charity whose objectives are: the relief of poverty and financial hardship, the advancement of education and religion, the relief of sickness, and the preservation of good health, in particular but not exclusively, in Rigul, Kham, Tibet.

Rigul, Tibet, is the homeland of Ringu Tulku Rinpoche where he has his monastery.

100% of all donations and proceeds from sales received by Rigul Trust will go to benefit the people of Rigul.

To find out more or to make a donation please visit:

www.rigultrust.org

info@rigultrust.org & donations@rigultrust

Patron: Ringu Tulku Rinpoche | Founder: Margaret Richardson

UK Charity Registration No: 1124076

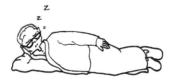

For an up to date list of books by Ringu Tulku,
please see the Books section at

www.bodhicharya.org

*Our professional skills are given free of charge in order to
produce these books, and Bodhicharya Publications is run
by volunteers; so your purchase of this book goes entirely to
fund further books and contribute to humanitarian and
educational projects supported by Bodhicharya.*

Milton Keynes UK
Ingram Content Group UK Ltd.
UKHW052017010224
436953UK00007B/74